Original title:
Ode to the Old Oak

Copyright © 2025 Creative Arts Management OÜ
All rights reserved.

Author: Harrison Blake
ISBN HARDBACK: 978-1-80567-223-4
ISBN PAPERBACK: 978-1-80567-522-8

A Heartwood Legacy

In a field where whispers play,
An old oak bloats by night and day.
Its branches wave, a merry dance,
Spying squirrels in a silly trance.

With acorns dropping like the rain,
Bouncing softly, causing pain.
"Watch your head!" the critters cry,
As they dodge the nature's pie in the sky.

Its bark's a map of ages past,
With carvings made to always last.
A love note here, a heart-shaped sign,
Romance under its limbs align.

The birds all gather for a show,
Auditions held on branches low.
With croaks and chirps, they take the stage,
In the bark's sweet laughter, they engage.

So here's to the tree with roots so wide,
Its leafy humor, our hearts can't hide.
In every giggle, we find our voice,
Under the oak, we all rejoice.

Sanctuary of the Wise

Underneath your sprawling arms,
Squirrels host their wildest charms.
Chattering tales of daring deeds,
While acorns fall, like tiny seeds.

Birds debate their morning songs,
Each one claims that they belong.
You simply laugh, with leaves so green,
A wiser tree has never been.

King of the Canopy

You wear a crown of twigs and leaves,
With sunny rays that dance and weave.
A jester chipmunk scurries round,
As you hold court, in silence crowned.

The sun bows low, your knightly glow,
While evening bees put on a show.
You chuckle low as shadows play,
In your grand realm, come what may.

Emblems of Resilience

Your gnarled limbs tell tales of old,
Of storms you've braved, and heat and cold.
With bark like armor, tough and true,
You stand so proud, with one main view.

While critters cling to every bough,
You wink and nod, and take a bow.
For every ring that adds a year,
You gain more laughs with every cheer.

The Embrace of Nature's Pillar

When winds blow strong and branches sway,
You bend and sway, come what may.
Your mighty trunk, both thick and wide,
Holds secrets deep, where fairies hide.

You dance with shadows, spin around,
For all who know, you wear the crown.
In every gust, you find a jest,
Oh, how you laugh, you golden jest!

Soliloquy of the Weathered Trunk

Oh, the squirrels come and go,
With acorns in their paws,
I'm the ancient stand, you know,
With bark that earns applause.

Birds in my branches swing,
Who knew I'd host a show?
I've heard all they can sing,
While I root down below.

The Legacy of Leaves

The leaves gossip with the breeze,
Saying, 'Look! There goes a cat!'
Falling like confetti, please!
Every season, just like that.

I shed them like a pet's hair,
They rustle loud with glee,
If only they'd become aware,
They've all got plans for tea.

Roots That Bind

Underground I make my way,
Twisting, turning, never straight,
Hiding secrets, night and day,
A tangled web, just call it fate.

Neighbors jog above my head,
While I sip on the ground's brew,
Dear friend, you may laugh instead,
But I'm laughing right with you!

The Canopy's Chorus

In the crown, it's quite a party,
Branches jiving left and right,
Even the sun joins the hearty,
Trying hard to shine so bright.

A raccoon plays the tambourine,
While owls keep the beat,
Nature's rhythm, quite the scene,
With roots tapping their own feet!

Embrace of the Wind

A mighty tree sways with grace,
Leaves laugh as they dance in place.
The branches wave, a silly tease,
Whispering secrets in the breeze.

Old roots chuckle, deep and wise,
While squirrels leap, a wild surprise.
A hammock hung, a cozy nook,
Where dreaming folks share their book.

The trunk stands firm, a sturdy friend,
With knots and bumps, its message send.
"Come climb aboard, swing like a kite,"
As wise old branches share delight.

The wind chips in, a playful breeze,
Tickling bark, it loves to tease.
Together they twirl, bounce, and spin,
In joyful dances, nature's grin.

In Tribute to Sturdy Branches

A trunk so broad, it needs a hat,
To keep the sun's glare off a cat.
With branches wide, like arms that greet,
Birds nestle in for a silent seat.

The squirrels race, a madcap chase,
Around the bark, they find their place.
With acorns dropped like little bombs,
The ground is stocked with nature's charms.

Old leaves gossip as they flip,
Spinning tales of their latest trip.
Each twig and bough, a jester dressed,
In nature's play, they seem the best.

Beneath the shade, picnics unfold,
With sandwiches and tales retold.
A sturdy friend in nature's play,
The tree declares it's here to stay.

Guardians of the Grove

In leafy halls where shadows dwell,
The old tree stands, it knows too well.
With branches crossed, like arms in care,
It guards the grove, a home so rare.

Watch out for owls in the night,
Their wise old eyes are quite the sight.
They hoot and holler from the nest,
Making sure all are safe and blessed.

The raccoons play, they scurry around,
In search of treasures on the ground.
While beetles march in socks of flair,
All gather round the old tree's lair.

Through seasons bright and storms that groan,
The oak stands tall, never alone.
A jester, king, in leafy cheer,
The grove's own guardian, year by year.

The Legacy of Ageless Boughs

A sprawling oak with stories vast,
Each knotted trunk holds tales from the past.
Its branches stretch like arms in jest,
Inviting all to join the quest.

A swing hangs high, kids jump with glee,
Squeals of laughter drift like a breeze.
With every creak, the boughs confess,
They've seen it all, no need to stress.

In autumn's splendor, leaves take flight,
Swirling down, like confetti bright.
The old oak chuckles, then bows low,
"I've still got moves! Just watch me grow!"

Through every season's vibrant dance,
It offers life, a true romance.
With jokes and jests, it spins its tale,
An ancient friend on every trail.

The Old Oak's Resilience

Beneath the hefty branches wide,
Squirrels plan their acorn pride,
With each shade they claim as theirs,
They throw nutty parties, unaware.

Storms may howl and winds may sway,
Still, the old oak stands to play,
With roots so deep, it holds the ground,
While branches dance, joyful and round.

Reflections Beneath the Boughs

Gathered folks with drinks in hand,
Crack jokes and laugh, it's quite a stand,
The old oak grins with leafy glee,
Hiding secrets, oh so free.

A bird once tried a comic act,
But tripped on branches, quite a fact,
Each giggle shakes the sturdy tree,
As laughter blooms like honeybee.

The Nature of Longevity

Years roll on like squirrels at play,
With each passing season, come what may,
The oak just rolls its knobby eyes,
As if to say, 'I've seen worse tries!'

Beneath its shade, the kids do run,
Playing catch, having fun,
The old oak chuckles, roots entwined,
With tales that leave the young ones blind.

Timorous Leaves and Timeless Tales

Leaves quiver gently in the breeze,
They tell stories with utmost ease,
About the times they swayed and shook,
And the owls who wrote the best of books.

A raccoon once made quite a scene,
Dressed in nuts, it was truly keen,
The laughter echoed through the wood,
For nature's quirks are understood.

A Crown of Green against the Sky

With branches wide, it struts around,
An ancient king in leafy crown.
It tickles clouds with jaunty glee,
While squirrels plot a heist of brie.

Its acorns drop with witty flair,
Each plop a joke that fills the air.
The passerby just shakes their head,
"That tree's off talking nonsense, dread!"

The Forgotten Tendrils of Time

What secrets lie in bark so grand?
Old tales of mischief at hand.
With creaks and groans, it starts to share,
A jest of youth, a windy dare.

Its limbs have danced in every breeze,
But now it sways with gentle tease.
To moments lost, it gives a wink,
"Oh, what a time! Let's have a drink!"

In Reverence to Nature's Monument

The wooden giant stands so tall,
A witness to the best and worst of all.
It chuckles when the storm clouds loom,
And shakes its leaves, "Bring on the gloom!"

Though people come with cameras bright,
It poses proudly, left and right.
With roots that grab the ground so tight,
It knows, in life, it's quite a sight!

Dance of the Dappled Light

Beneath the cloak of leafy shade,
The sunlight winks, a playful trade.
The leaves all shimmer in delight,
As bugs perform their tiny flight.

It's nature's stage, where shadows prance,
While beetles try to steal a glance.
A dance that makes no sense at all,
Yet in this grove, we hear the call!

Whispers of the Ancient Canopy

In the park where you stand tall,
Your branches dance, they never fall.
Squirrels gossip, nuts in tow,
Under your shade, the world moves slow.

With knots and curls, your bark's a tale,
Of storms you've faced and winds that wail.
Your leaves chuckle at the passing breeze,
As you sip rain like a fine, aged cheese.

You've seen love, laughter, and a dog named Fred,
Who thought your roots were a perfect bed.
Each twist and turn of your mighty frame,
Is a story told in nature's name.

Beneath your feet, the ground they dig,
For treasure hidden beneath the fig.
With humor wrapped in every grain,
You're both wise and wacky, serene and insane.

The Timeworn Guardian

Oh guardian of the picnic spree,
With ants and crumbs, so joyous and free.
You oversee all the fun and games,
While birds relay your quirky names.

Your limbs, a stage for feathery clowns,
As kids play king while wearing crowns.
You nod to daisies growing near,
And giggle softly, as if to sneer.

Each autumn, your costume's a riot,
In orange, red, you start a diet.
Yet winter comes and you wear white,
And still you manage to look quite bright.

Around your trunk, we play and spin,
You watch, amused, as we jump in.
Though time has woven its intricate net,
Your spirit, dear friend, we shan't forget.

Echoes of Leaves Long Past

In whispering tones, the leaves unite,
Chattering secrets in the moonlight.
Conversations of ages playfully swirl,
With whispers of acorns and nature's twirl.

You've seen fashions come and go,
In your ancient arms, the trends all flow.
Boys in shorts and girls with braids,
Under you, the young heart parades.

When storms roll in, you sway and sway,
While critters cling to you in dismay.
Yet come the sun, you spread your arms,
Enticing sunbeams with all your charms.

In summer's warmth, our laughter blends,
With tales of how the oak tree bends.
You hold our joy in your leafy bushel,
As we celebrate life, giggles and huzzah!

Embrace of the Gnarled Roots

Oh roots that twist like curly fries,
You give the critters a place to hide.
Tangled together, a merry band,
In your embrace, we take our stand.

You tease the lawnmowers that dare roam,
With snickers of grass that call you home.
While flowers bloom in bright array,
You dance a jig each sunny day.

How many snacks have fallen your way?
Banana peels from picnics at play.
Yet never complain, you just enjoy,
When crumbs descend from each laughing boy.

And as we gather 'neath your spread,
We tell our tales of joy instead.
A gnarled embrace, so funny, so nice,
In nature's park, you add a slice.

Gentle Giants and the Songs They Sing

Roots so deep, trunk so wide,
Swaying leaves, a leafy ride.
Here comes the squirrel, quick and spry,
Chasing shadows as birds fly by.

Bouncing branches, a dance so grand,
Branches shake like a marching band.
Forgetful branches lost in their thoughts,
Hum a tune of the mischief they've sought.

Twisting tales in the summer breeze,
Napping critters in the sun with ease.
The acorns drop like tiny bombs,
Tiny mammals jump and perform their charms.

Swaying softly 'neath the bright blue sky,
Giggling leaves as they sway and sigh.
Oh, what a life they have to sing,
In this tree, oh the joy they bring!

Beneath the Treetops

Twirling squirrels with acorn hats,
Stealing snacks from lazy cats.
Whispering secrets in breezy rhymes,
Chasing shadows through passing times.

Frolicking geese in a silly fight,
Wobbling branches from day to night.
Dancing shadows, a playful crew,
Under the sunbeam's golden hue.

A comedy show within the bark,
Nature's laughter ignites a spark.
The old oak chuckles with each new joke,
As branches bend, then rise and poke.

Who knew trees had such flair and grace?
In the forest, it's a lively place.
Beneath the treetops, joy is supreme,
Where laughter flows like a bubbling stream.

Life Unfolds

Once a sprout, now a towering tale,
Waving goodbyes to a lazy snail.
Gnarled branches don quirky caps,
Fuzzy squirrels create fun mishaps.

Each knot a story, each leaf a song,
A comedy act that lasts so long.
Hidden treasures in the bark's embrace,
Oh, the secrets that find their space.

Nutty antics all day and night,
Bouncing buddies in playful flight.
Life unfolds in patches of cheer,
With branches laughing, "We're glad you're here!"

Windy tales of the breeze's prance,
In this grand theater, life's a dance.
Old oak, you cradle each moment bright,
In laughter's glow, everything feels right!

The Watcher of the Whispering Woods

Sitting still like a wise old sage,
Watching critters run the playful stage.
A jackrabbit slips, and the leaves all cheer,
Oh, what a ruckus, let's watch them near!

Mischief abounds, it's a sneaky show,
Giggling chipmunks and a crow named Joe.
He boasts of secrets that make them roll,
Cackling loudly, he plays his role.

The whispers of wind pass on the joke,
As branches shimmy and chuckle, awoke.
Tall and proud, what a view so grand,
The watcher smiles at the goofy band.

In this enchanted, waggish glade,
Laughter echoes, no plans are made.
Just moments of joy in the subtle light,
In the serendipity of day and night.

Cradle of Memory Under the Sky

In a cradle of shade and laughter bright,
Memories flutter like leaves in flight.
Beneath the branches, a whimsical sight,
As critters join in, taking their bite.

The old oak grins, with wisdom to share,
Mischief and mayhem float in the air.
Rustling leaves, a secretive chatter,
In the forest's heart, it's all that matters.

Under the sky, where silliness replays,
A parade of wonder in endless ways.
Nutty escapades, fables unfold,
In the sun's warm embrace, dreams are bold.

So here's to the laughter when memories flow,
To the magic of moments as breezes blow.
In this cradle, peace and fun intertwine,
A tapestry of joy, woven divine.

Within the Whispered Winds

Beneath the branches, squirrels play,
Chasing shadows through the day.
Acorns drop like clumsy bombs,
Upon the ground, oh how it calms.

The leaves gossip in a breeze,
Sharing secrets with such ease.
It seems the bark just rolled its eyes,
At all our silly human sighs.

Old roots dig deep, a steadfast friend,
In this dance, there's no clear end.
Who knew a tree could be so wise?
It's got more tales than our goodbyes.

So let us raise a cup to thee,
Our leafy friend, all proud and free.
You've stood through storms and silly pranks,
With laughter in your sturdy thanks.

An Elegy for the Leafy Giants

Oh mighty giants, you've seen it all,
From morning sun to evening's fall.
With branches stretching, you seem to grin,
While birds build nests, and squirrels spin.

In winter's chill, you wear white caps,
Yet poke fun at our hasty naps.
Your bark may wrinkle, but oh so spry,
You still dance to the wind, oh my!

We'll tell our tales of leaf and root,
As we munch on your acorns, oh what a hoot!
Your trunk may be thick, but your humor flows,
In your shadow, the laughter grows.

So here's to you, dear giants bold,
Your funny quirks, a story told.
In every creak, and every sway,
Your punchlines land, come what may.

Solace in the Shade

Under your arms, a cool embrace,
Where picnics bloom in dappled grace.
But watch your sandwiches, don't let them stray,
The ants are hungry, come what may!

Your shadows dance in the warm sun's light,
Inviting joy, a pure delight.
When summer's heat becomes a beast,
You're our haven, our leafy feast.

Stories told beneath your gaze,
Of youthful days and silly ways.
The laughter echoes, the memories cling,
While birds in chorus begin to sing.

So here's to our refuge, steadfast and grand,
A twist of humor at your command.
In the fabric of time, you're woven tight,
Oh, how you make our spirits light!

A Chronicle Bound by Time

In your presence, history thrives,
With each ring telling us wild lives.
The whispers of ages float on air,
A chatty trunk, with long tales to share.

When storms come crashing, you just sway,
Laughing off the worries of the day.
Nature's chuckles echo in your leaves,
As you shake off care like a dog that cleaves.

You've seen us grow, you've seen us fall,
Through every season, you've heard the call.
While we all fret over days gone by,
You stand like a meme, oh so spry!

So let's write a story, both quirky and bright,
Of roots and branches reaching to the height.
In every gnarled twist, a giggle found,
Together we stand, forever unbound.

A Testament of Time

Beneath your shade, the squirrels play,
You've seen a hundred picnic days.
With acorns dropped like tiny bombs,
You laugh at nature's silly charms.

You stand so tall, you old wise tree,
While folks just groan, 'Is that a bee?'
Your branches wiggle, twist and shout,
And all the birds just fly about.

Each ring you hold, a tale to tell,
Of windy storms and sunshine swell.
You've got the gossip from the creek,
In whispers shared by every freak.

So here's to you, oh giant trunk,
You've got more bark than that old punk.
Together we'll joke 'til it's night,
And hope the moon's not too bright!

Stories Written in Bark

Oh, look at you, with age and grace,
A history written, a timeless place.
Your bark's a scrapbook of tales gone by,
Of woodpecker tap-dances and clouds that sigh.

Every wound you wear tells a comical plight,
Of raccoons who thought they could sneak by at night.
With laughter echoing in your hollowed log,
You keep secrets of each playful frog.

In your branches, mischief abounds,
As children climb, and laughter resounds.
You host the best treehouse dreams,
Where every kid hears wild moonbeams.

So raise your branches to silly songs,
To twirling winds and where joy belongs.
Here's to stories held so tight,
In every groove, in morning light!

Reverie Among the Branches

Swinging high upon your limbs we go,
Where squirrels chatter and breezes blow.
Your leafy arms, a canopy wide,
Hide giggles of folks who just can't hide.

You sway with stories of all things bright,
From fluttering butterflies to owl's late flight.
Each rustling leaf has a punchline to share,
In the mystery of your aged air.

Let's dance with shadows, sing with glee,
As jazzing sunlight winks at me.
Your knotted roots twist like old jokes told,
In laughter's embrace, as tales unfold.

So here beneath your boughs we stay,
Where whimsy drifts like the autumn sway.
To dream amidst your playful sway,
Silly moments make today!

The Heartbeat of the Forest

Oh mighty tree, with a heartbeat strong,
You dance with the winds in a playful song.
Your trunk's a drum, your leaves the cheer,
While critters gather round to hear.

In sunny patches, laughter spills,
Of cotton candy clouds and climbing thrills.
From acorn hats to ghosts of bark,
You cradle the joy, the light, the spark.

Under your watch, time takes a pause,
With giggles echoing, oh what a cause!
You wear a crown of bird's delight,
In the lullabies from day to night.

So let us dance the forest beat,
With every stomp, a joyous feat.
Your roots hold stories deep as the night,
As laughter twirls in soft moonlight!

Beacons of Serenity

In the garden stands a tree,
With branches wide and leaves carefree.
It sways and dances, oh so spry,
A rustling whisper, just nearby.

Its acorns drop, like little bombs,
Causing squirrels to yell, "Oh, psst!" and chomp.
They scamper round, a lively crew,
While birds hold meetings, yes, it's true.

With trunks so thick, it won't give ground,
It chuckles softly, knows it's crowned.
A beacon bright for those who pass,
A gnarled old sage with tons of sass.

In summer's heat, it throws a shade,
A hammock swings, where dreams are laid.
The kids all climb, and bark they peel,
As laughter echoes, joy's the deal.

In the Shade of Wisdom

There's wisdom in the twisted bark,
A gossip tree, bright as a lark.
It's seen the years, both wild and tame,
And giggles softly at the game.

With every breeze, a story's told,
Of squirrels bold, and tales of old.
They gather close, for a good chat,
While nearby, flowers laugh at that.

When lightning strikes, it stands its ground,
It shakes it off, no worries found.
With roots that dance beneath the earth,
It knows its worth, it knows its worth.

All creatures pause, in shade's embrace,
A place where laughter wins the race.
In the quiet, wisdom flows,
With every heart, delight it sows.

Legacy Woven in Roots

Beneath the soil, the secrets lie,
In tangled roots, a family tie.
The oak is wise, it winks with glee,
As critters race, shout, "Look at me!"

A legacy of tiny seeds,
That sprout to dance, fulfill their needs.
While squirrels collect their winter stash,
The oak looks on, with a hearty laugh.

Its branches sway, like hands in cheer,
Encouraging dreams, drawing near.
Those roots entwined, they hold the ground,
A patchwork of life, connections found.

When autumn comes, the leaves all fall,
The children play, and heed the call.
A swirling carpet, bright and bold,
With giggles wrapped in tales of old.

The Emblem of Endurance

A sturdy oak, oh what a sight,
Through stormy days and starry nights.
It stands its ground, with knotted pride,
While others sway, and some decide.

To shelter all, in its embrace,
While picnics thrive, it's heaven's place.
With patches of moss, a comfy seat,
It entertains with roots so neat.

Old branches creak, but they won't break,
It's seen enough to know what's fake.
It laughs at clouds, and shakes the rain,
A weathered friend, who feels no pain.

When winter chills, it dons a dress,
Of frosty flakes — oh, what a mess!
Yet come the spring, it shines once more,
An emblem strong, a legend's core.

A Sanctuary Among the Leaves

In the shade of your limbs, I find my retreat,
Squirrels plotting schemes, oh what a feat!
Your branches like arms cradle the sun,
I sip lemonade, laughing—oh, what fun!

Under your canopy, the world feels at peace,
While chipmunks and robins never cease,
To gossip and chatter about the day's news,
In this leafy kingdom, I lose all my blues.

Under the Arch of Ages

Oh, wise old friend, with stories to tell,
You've seen the seasons, and all that befell.
Your bark wears wrinkles like a wise old sage,
I swear you've seen eeny-meeny miny-moe age!

Here children climb high, like monkeys in flight,
Pretending to be kings, surveying the height.
Your branches are their thrones, their rapid delight,
You grin with each giggle—what a wondrous sight!

The Oak's Silent Soliloquy

You stand with dignity, not a word from you,
While whispers of breezes carry tales so true.
Each rustle a giggle, each leaf a quip,
As I ponder your thoughts, my imagination skips.

I wonder if you chuckle at clouds floating past,
Or sigh at the years, moving ever so fast.
Maybe you giggle at squirrels on a spree,
Your laughter echoes softly—you clever old tree!

Emblems of Eternity

With acorns like jewels, you crown the ground,
While ants march in lines, a parade all around.
Oh, your knotted old trunk holds secrets galore,
Like how many times you've seen a bird soar.

Your leafy attire sways with a flair,
And I can't help but grin at the whimsy in air.
For amidst all your wisdom, humor remains,
In the dance of your branches when the soft wind complains.

Veins of the Old Oak

Branches reach, a giant hat,
Squirrels race, and where's the cat?
Twigs like fingers, scratching sky,
Leaves dance like they're saying hi.

In winter coats of snow so bright,
Old Oak chuckles, 'What a sight!'
While birds compete for best parade,
He shakes his bark, they're all delayed.

Roots like noodles, thick and wide,
"Watch your step!" the critters chide.
Knots and bumps, a wrinkled face,
"Too much sun, I need my space!"

With every storm, he sways and sways,
A proud old friend through sunny days.
His laughter echoes, wise and bold,
In whispers sweet, his tales are told.

A Sanctuary of Silence

Where the world buzzes quick and fast,
Stands a haven from the blast.
Old Oak winks, with patience grand,
'Join my shade, just take my hand.'

Here the bumblebees take a chance,
Bouncing 'round in a goofy dance.
With acorns dropping like confetti,
All the woodland creatures ready.

Sitting still, you'll hear the wise,
Crickets chirp their lullabies.
A squirrel sneezes, takes a dive,
And nature giggles, all alive.

Underneath, the laughter swells,
Listen close, can you tell?
The old tree's jokes and tales galore,
In this silence, we want more.

Telling Tales in Tranquil Shadows

In the shade where secrets sleep,
Old Oak whispers, not too deep.
His knots and gnarls a tapestry,
"Gather 'round, come hear from me."

"Once I fought a storm so bold,
With wind and rain, I'm proud and old.
But the best part? A birdy pledge,
Each year I'm crowned a wobbly hedge!"

With roots so twisted, tales are spun,
Of a mischievous raccoon's run.
He juggled acorns, took a fall,
And cats still talk of that great brawl.

In tranquil shadows, laughter reigns,
As grasshoppers fill the air with strains.
Old Oak smiles, a wise old chap,
"Life's much better with a laugh!"

A Thousand Years Beneath the Sky

A thousand years, the wise old tree,
Says, "I'm young; it's you, not me!"
With tangles of lichen and bark,
He stands there with a wry little smirk.

Each season spins its silly game,
From sweet spring blooms to autumn's fame.
Oh, look at that squirrel with its nut!
He's got style, oh, what a cut!

With stories that twist like vines so thick,
He chuckles at time's little trick.
"Who has the better sense of fun?
The tree or the bunny? Place your pun!"

So raise a glass to the roots so deep,
To the joyful moments that we keep.
Under the sky, forever so spry,
Here's to laughter until we fly!

Timeworn Majesty

With branches wide, an ancient show,
The old oak grins, a King in tow.
His neighbors sigh in envy's song,
While squirrels leap and dance along.

His bark, a patchwork quilt of years,
Has hosted laughter, joys, and tears.
The kids play tag around his base,
While he just chuckles at the chase.

In autumn's glow, his leaves do twirl,
As if they dance, a crazy whirl.
He takes the gusts with regal flair,
"I'm the grandest, who would dare?"

He cracks a joke 'neath moonlit air,
"Why grow up? I just don't care!"
With roots so deep, he won't take flight,
In nature's circus, he's delight!

The Old Friend in the Forest

In a glade where shadows creep,
An old oak stands, and laughs in sleep.
He tells the trees, "I've seen it all,
Like wayward squirrels who think they're small."

Beneath his arms, the creatures play,
Birds play poker, or so they say.
He rolls his eyes as meetings start,
"Can't we just nap? Let's skip the art!"

The rabbits bounce and snicker loud,
While deer and foxes form a crowd.
With wisdom deep, he makes a pun,
"Oh dear, it's time for more fun!"

And when the raindrops tap his crown,
He bellows, "Hey! Don't bring me down!"
A friend to all, both firm and wise,
This old oak thrives beneath the skies.

A Home for the Untold

In his embrace, the stories wait,
Of cheeky critters, love, and fate.
Hollowed sides with secrets packed,
What tales are spun when the sun's intact?

A raccoon slinks to tale so bold,
"Living here, I'm never cold!"
A ghostly squirrel, a tale begins,
"Last week I lost my prized acorns!"

The owls chuckle, under moonlit gaze,
"Who needs the news? We're wise and hazed."
Old oak just laughs, his branches shake,
"What's life without a little break?"

With every setting sun he knows,
New stories bloom where laughter flows.
So gather round, folks, young and old,
His heart beats deep—a home for the untold!

Symphony of Rings

Beneath his cloak of leaves so wide,
The old oak breathes with spirits inside.
Each ring a page from years gone by,
A symphony played 'neath the vast sky.

He sways to whispers of the breeze,
And jokes with leaves, "Just chill with ease!"
As squirrels argue, he takes a bow,
"No need for fighting, just share the chow!"

Seasons march, and he hums along,
A maestro in nature's endless song.
Birds chirp in harmony, what a crew,
"On today's menu, a worm for you!"

While splashes of rain fall in queues,
He strums the raindrops, "Let's dance, it's true!"
With age comes wisdom, laughter's key,
This old oak's tune is wild and free!

Oak-Litten Stories

In the shade where squirrels play,
A leafy stage led the way.
The old oak shook with laughter loud,
As whispered secrets formed a crowd.

With acorns dropped like mishaps grand,
They bounced like heads at a rock band.
The bark began to tell a joke,
And giggles stirred in every oak.

A raccoon danced, what a sight!
He twirled around in morning light.
By twilight, tales of giants grew,
In every twist, an oak's debut.

So gather 'round, you curious folk,
Join merry tales from this old oak.
With each jest and crafty pun,
Nature's humor weighs a ton!

Hearth of Nature's Embrace

On a carpet of leaves so bright,
The old tree warms the frosty night.
A chubby raccoon with mischief bakes,
Cookies made from acorns and flakes.

The owl plays DJ from a high perch,
With beats so smooth, they make you lurch.
Beneath the oak, a party swells,
With critters dancing, casting spells.

A hedgehog showed off quirky moves,
While crickets stomped with furry grooves.
The moonlight twinkled just in time,
To catch the rhythm, oh so prime!

So raise a glass of dew drops cheer,
To nature's hearth, we gather near.
With laughter shared 'neath branches wide,
In the warmth of leaves, let joy abide!

A Tapestry of Time in Gnarled Grasp

This old fellow with wrinkles deep,
Holds stories in knots with secrets to keep.
With branches like arms, he waves hello,
To every wanderer, high and low.

He recalls a time when he was spry,
Back then he touched the clear blue sky.
Now he's a sage with humor bright,
Guiding lost passers with delight.

The squirrels love to play the game,
Of hide and seek, they're quite the same.
Around his roots they scamper fast,
In a frenzy that never seems to last.

So let's clink our nuts and share a laugh,
At the wise old oak's enchanted path.
With stories spun from every branch,
We'll dance with joy, take a chance!

Remnants of Raindrops Past

When raindrops leap from leafy heights,
   The old oak wears its jewelry bright.
With every droplet, a giggle springs,
   Tickling bark as the willow sings.

"Did you hear the one about the sky?"
As thunder chuckles, weep not, oh my!
For in this forest, laughter's the game,
   And oak's glory is never to blame.

With puddles deep like nature's pools,
   Wet feet turn into joyful tools.
Children splash down, giggles afloat,
   As the tree hums a merry note.

So gather round, let laughter dance,
   Join the rain's whimsical romance.
For in the old oak's boughs so wide,
Life's playful heart finds nowhere to hide!

Legacy in Every Leaf's Vein

A tree in the forest, never a bore,
With leaves that dance, and roots that snore.
He tells the tales of a thousand years,
While squirrels giggle and whispers of peers.

His acorns drop, with comedic flair,
A hat for the critters, quite the affair.
They tumble and roll, like a slapstick scene,
Every nut a joke, even to the unseen.

Birds tweet their tunes, a symphony bright,
While branches wave gently, a wobbly sight.
Old Oak chuckles, with his bark all gnarled,
He's the king of the woods, happily snarl'd.

So raise up a glass to that wise old trunk,
With humor and heart, he's far from a punk.
For every leaf's vein, he's telling a tale,
Of laughter and joy that will always prevail.

Guardianship of the Greenwood

In the heart of the woods, stands a fellow quite proud,
An old oak who thinks he's the wisest in the crowd.
With a grin made of bark and a tangle of vines,
He watches over nature, drinking sunlight like wine.

The rabbits convene for a council most grand,
To ask for advice from their leafy old friend.
"Tell us, dear Oak, how do we outsmart,
The fox who is sly and has a big heart?"

"Well, hop high and low, and then binky like mad,
Just avoid my old roots, or you'll surely feel bad!"
The old oak chuckles, as they scurry away,
An entertainer too, but he won't take the pay!

So there he will stand, in his leafy domain,
A guardian of laughter, in sunshine and rain.
With every wise crack, he makes nature grin,
Our beloved old oak, where the fun will begin.

Standing Tall Through Storms

With winds howling loud, and the skies painted gray,
The old oak stands firm, in a comical way.
He sways to and fro, but never does break,
"You call this a storm? Oh, bless my old flake!"

His branches may shake, and his leaves might yell,
But he laughs at the thunder, "Is that all you can tell?"
As rain slicks his bark, he shimmies right on,
A dance of delight, from dusk until dawn.

The birds hold their breath, nestled snug in their nests,
While squirrels make bets on this unyielding jest.
"I'll take two acorns!" says one with a grin,
"That old oak can take it! He's known for the win!"

As the tempest draws near, he's a merry old chap,
Spinning tales to the critters, who rest on his lap.
Through gusts and gales, he stands proud and silly,
An emblem of laughter, even when chilly.

Nature's Enchanted Tower

An ancient old tree, a tower of glee,
With branches like arms, hugging the sky's spree.
Creatures come calling, to scale his rough walls,
In pursuit of the snacks that his acorns befall.

With a belly that rumbles, he shakes with delight,
As squirrels party hard, from morning to night.
"Come one, come all!" he scoffs with a laugh,
"Grab some lunch from my shade; I'm your leafy half!"

The rabbits play tag, around roots all a-twist,
While birds chirp a tune that you surely can't miss.
The sun casts a glow on this whimsical knight,
In the court of the woodland, where laughter takes flight.

So here's to that tower, with his crown of green flair,
He's not just a tree; he's a friend with great care.
In the forest of mirth, where every heart sings,
Nature's enchanted tower gives joy on the wings.

Shadows of the Timeless

Beneath the branches, squirrels play,
They plot all night, by light of day.
A game of tag, they dart and weave,
Who knew a tree could make us grieve?

A shadow here, a shadow there,
The old oak's wisdom, oh so rare.
"Do branches droop with years?" I ask,
"Or is it just my growing flask?"

The squirrels chuckle, gather round,
While acorns from the branches abound.
"Who's the king of this leafy throne?"
The old oak whispers, "I'm alone!"

We laugh as echoes fill the air,
With laughter, leaves begin to share.
Yet, when the wind starts to conspire,
The branches sway and dreams retire.

A Dance of Seasons

Each fall a leaf does take a trip,
Spinning down with a graceful flip.
The tree just smiles, it knows what's true,
New buds will burst—like me and you!

Winter's chill brings a frosty glance,
Sure, the squirrels now wear a pants!
They shiver, twitch, but dance away,
In the old oak's arms, they plan to play.

Spring arrives, with blooms galore,
"Hey tree," they shout, "dance once more!"
But roots just groan and branches sway,
"Keep your party, I'll nap today!"

Summer blooms with sunshine's glee,
Ants marching up—oh, what a spree!
The old oak chuckles with each breeze,
As creatures scamper with such ease.

The Breath of Ancient Wood

A deep breath whispers through the leaves,
A gentle laugh, the old oak heaves.
"What's that?" asks Chipmunk, ears a-flap,
"Just tales of old, in nature's map."

The tree, it claims, once wore a crown,
All the squirrels gathered around:
"Tell us, tree, about your youth!"
"Too many rings, too much uncouth!"

With every breeze, a story's told,
About the knights and treasures bold.
"Did you see dragons?" a young one squeaks,
"Just some bad jokes from passing peaks!"

As twilight falls and shadows play,
The oak just grins in a funny way.
"I've seen it all, the joy and fear,
But mostly, I've seen you folks here!"

Heritage of the Green Giant

Born from a seed, with dreams so wide,
The old oak grew with branches as pride.
"Your family tree, it's quite a mess,"
A squirrel snickers, "What a jest!"

With roots entwined, a history shows,
Of fuzzy hats and forgotten toes.
"What's the secret?" the ants inquire,
"Just stay grounded, nothing to aspire!"

Branches wave like arms in flight,
"Dance with me, it feels so right!"
But one lone branch, a grumpy one,
Sighs, "I prefer a quieter fun."

Oh, what a dynasty, tall and wide,
With tales of acorns and critters' pride.
The green giant laughs as shadows blend,
For every tree has fun to lend!

Veins of the Earth

Roots deep in the giggling ground,
Tickling worms all year round.
Branches dance with gusty flair,
Leaves gossip, if they dare.

Woodpeckers drum a silly tune,
Claiming the tree as their saloon.
Squirrels in a nutty race,
Chasing shadows, just in case.

Bark worn smooth from winters past,
Fallen acorns, a crunchy blast.
Every tale the oak could tell,
Would make even grumpy folks yell!

In shadows where children play,
Sharing secrets that won't sway.
With each twist and turn they take,
The old oak laughs at every shake.

The Oak's Lament

Once stood tall with leafy pride,
Now it's just a branchy ride.
Acorns drop like comedic bombs,
Knocking hats off heads like psalms.

Bragging squirrels with fancy flair,
Strut around without a care.
Branches creak like old guitars,
Rolling laughter, played on bars.

Every breeze a gentle tease,
That sends the autumn leaves to sneeze.
A tree can't put on fancy shoes,
But still, it wears the best of hues.

Come stroll under its leafy hug,
Where gossip flies, like a snug bug.
Listen close, the secrets keep,
As the old oak takes its leap.

Seasons of Solitude

Springtime brings ridiculous blooms,
Dancing flowers in friendly rooms.
Summer's sun, a blazing prank,
Painting shadows in the bank.

Autumn's laugh is crisp and flash,
Leaves come tumbling with a splash.
Winter grumbles, huddles tight,
With snowflakes giggling, quite a sight.

A tree that stands through thick and thin,
With roots that hold like they won a win.
While critters joke and chase their dreams,
The old oak chuckles, bursting seams.

A spectacle of nature's jest,
Through each season, it feels blessed.
In solitude, it finds a crowd,
Funny tales, both soft and loud.

Life Amidst the Hallowed

A majestic giant with stories to share,
It winks at the moon with a bold, funny flair.
Amidst solemn shadows, it stands so tall,
A jester of wood in the grandest hall.

Squirrels dress in quirky attire,
While the oak sits by the fire.
Underneath, the grass tells tales,
Of epic fights between tiny snails.

Hallowed grounds of laughter ring,
Where little birds take up to swing.
In every rustle, a giggle heard,
As wind tickles each soft word.

So here it stands with twinkle and grace,
Offering shade, a warm embrace.
Life beneath its watchful glance,
Whispers secrets, leads the dance.

Whispered Histories in Quietude

Beneath the boughs where squirrels play,
Old tales swirl in bright array.
A acorn fell, and here it grew,
Who knew that dreams would form a crew?

With wise old limbs that dance with glee,
They wink at passers, oh so free.
The wind, it carries secrets low,
While birds audition for the show.

A bearded branch, quite full of sass,
Claims he was once a fancy class.
A leaf will chuckle from the height,
And whisper, "I'm the leafy knight!"

So gather 'round, both young and old,
For stories from the ancient gold.
An oak, you see, has much to share,
Just don't get lost in its dark hair!

The Old Oak's Embrace

In the meadow, he makes his stand,
A crooked grin by nature's hand.
With bark that's gnarled like grandpa's face,
He'll give you shade, a warm embrace!

His roots are tangled like a joke,
Sometimes they trip all who invoke.
A family of critters makes their bed,
In branches that seem to laugh instead.

When autumn comes, he wears a crown,
Of colors bright, not one brown down.
He waves his arms, a jolly sight,
A funny dance, he takes to flight!

So if you seek a cheerful friend,
Just lean against him, and pretend.
The old oak sways, a merry soul,
In every breeze, he plays the role!

Canopy of Dreams

Up above, a leafy quilt,
Where sunbeams thread with shadows built.
The branches gossip, quite a show,
Each rustle sends a giggle low.

What dreams drift through this leafy sea?
A longing for sweet jubilee.
The woodland creatures watch in awe,
As tales unfold without a flaw.

A squirrel in shades, a fashion feat,
Struts along on nimble feet.
He tips his hat, a charming lad,
But silly oaks, they just get mad!

Together beneath this arching dome,
We find our laughter call it home.
And every shade holds stories spun,
In chortles and chuckles, we become one!

Emblems of the Endless Heart

With every ring, a birthday cheer,
Old oak's heart beats loud and clear.
He counts the years through storms and sun,
Each branch a tale, a life begun.

Beehives thrumming in his chest,
Invite the pollen party guests.
While ants parade on trails of pride,
Declaring, "Here we waltz and glide!"

He winks at clouds, a cheeky mate,
And whispers jokes to those who wait.
"Why did the leaf break up?" he grins,
"Because it found new roots, not sins!"

So raise a glass to this grand sage,
Whose laughter echoes through the age.
An old oak stands, a humorous start,
Emblems of joy, an endless heart!

Memories in the Shade

Under branches wide and stout,
Squirrels dance round about.
With acorns flying through the air,
I dodge one with a startled stare.

The kids climb high, they yell and shout,
While I lie here, worn out.
"Be careful up there!" I call in jest,
"The ground's just fine, but you need rest!"

Each summer brings its fair delight,
Sunshine, laughter, pure delight.
Yet when autumn's leaves do fall,
I laugh—who needs a swimming pool at all?

So here I sit, in leafy cloak,
An old tree with a subtle joke.
With roots that burrow like ancient lore,
I wave my branches, "Come play some more!"

The Silent Sentinel

In the yard, I stand so grand,
A leafy giant, quite well-planned.
Neighbors whisper, as they pass,
"Is he a tree or a green-brushed mass?"

Birds perch high and gossip near,
I catch their tales, loud and clear.
"He's ancient! Wise! Can't move at all!"
Sure, I may not dance, but I won't fall!

The mailman trips over the roots,
While I just sway in my leafy boots.
"He clucks and clatters; oh, what a fuss!"
I chuckle softly, all aboard the bus!

Yet when dusk paints the skies anew,
I stand still, wearing my evening hue.
With a wink to the stars, I cheer each night,
"A silent sentinel, in the moonlight!"

Beneath the Boughs of Wisdom

Gather 'round, my little friends,
Under my limbs, the fun never ends.
With stories tangled in each leaf,
I share the tales of joyful grief.

The wise old owl perched high above,
Sings ballads of mischief and love.
"Who cooks dinner, who does the chores?"
The deer just nod, while washing their shores.

A picnic spread beneath my shade,
Sandwiches wrapped, lemonade made.
"Oh, tell me more!" the children plead,
I grin, "Yes, but only if you feed!"

As the sun dips low, I watch them play,
In whispers of night, they drift away.
Yet here I stay, with wisdom untold,
An ancient confessor, brave and bold.

Tranquil Majesty

Look at me, a tree so grand,
With leaves like hands that wave and stand.
The wind, my friend, plays hide and seek,
"Not now! I'm busy!" I silently squeak.

I wear a crown of twigs and vines,
Where birds make nests for future shrines.
"Excuse me, are you open for business?"
The chipmunks ask between their fitness.

A hammock strung from branch to branch,
I keep it swaying, give folks a chance.
"Oh dear! Don't fall!" they laugh and squeal,
While I stand steady, it's part of the deal.

So here I sway, with a breezy flair,
A tranquil giant, beyond compare.
With roots held tight in earthen dance,
Under my watch, there's always a chance.

Chronicles of the Verdant Elder

In the shade of your leafy arms,
Squirrels plan their little heists,
Stealing acorns, tossing charms,
While you rumble, giving some jests.

Mighty branches stretch and yawn,
A morning stretch that makes me grin,
You sway to a springtime song,
While birds await their chance to win.

Your trunk's got more knots than my socks,
Each one tells a tale so bizarre,
Of laughing kids and tricky knocks,
You keep those secrets, like a star.

And when the wind becomes a tease,
You shake your leaves like a grand dance,
Oh elder tree, with such great ease,
You make our world a carefree prance.

Sentinel of Forgotten Tales

Old and wise, you stand so grand,
With bark that looks like ancient scrolls,
Whispering stories, hand in hand,
With critters, thieves, and playful trolls.

An owl hoots, like a stand-up star,
While squirrels gather for some laughs,
Mice plot pranks, oh my, so bizarre,
You chuckle at their foolish crafts.

Upon your head, a bird takes flight,
Her singing voice, a feathered jest,
While you chuckle as day turns night,
And fireflies blink like they're blessed.

You sway like dancers, quite the sight,
A guardian of all things silly,
Your branches dancing left and right,
In the forest, you're the life of the lily.

A Dance of Light and Shadows

In your crown, the sunlight plays,
Casting shadows, shapes so rare,
A cat just pounced, oh what a craze,
You chuckle with a leafy flair.

Around your roots, a party brews,
Rabbits hopping, squirrels on edges,
You wiggle, tease them in their shoes,
While hidden critters weave their pledges.

With a gust, your leaves break into song,
Conducting the forest's daily jest,
Even the weather can't get it wrong,
Join the rhythm, it's all a fest!

For each twist and turn in your sway,
Echoes laughter far and near,
The woodland scene in grand ballet,
A dazzling show, worth every cheer.

The Heartbeat of the Forest

Oh mighty tree with heart so true,
The forest's pulse, you thump and beat,
With each rustle, you know what's due,
    A riddle game is set so sweet.

Your branches sway to nature's tune,
While raccoons gather, plotting schemes,
You chuckle softly, a wise old rune,
Decoding their mischievous dreams.

The wind whispers jokes, you laugh aloud,
While leaves twirl down like confetti bright,
You wear autumn's cloak, so proud,
    Every color, a pure delight!

Among the wild, you rule as king,
The laughter blooms in every space,
With you around, the forest sings,
    In happiness, we find our place.

Beneath the Gnarled Canopy

Underneath the twisted branches,
Squirrels plot their acorn heists,
While birds sing off-key ballads,
Critters clash in feathery feasts.

Beneath the leaves that shade the ground,
A debate on who's the king,
A rabbit claims it's obvious,
While a tortoise just does his thing.

With each gust of windy laughter,
The old oak shakes its mighty head,
"You think you own this grassy patch?"
"I've outlived all your woodland threads!"

So gather 'round, dear woodland friends,
And toast to this grand tree so wise,
For every giggle shared in shade,
With roots that reach towards the skies.

Stories Held in Bark

Etched in lines of ancient wisdom,
The oak holds tales both weird and wild,
Of lovers lost and squirrels' mischief,
Of a dog's chase, and the boy who smiled.

If trees could talk, they'd spill the tea,
About the rain that danced with glee,
And how that bee, so bold and brash,
Stole the nectar in a flash.

Each ring a year, each groove a grin,
Hiding the secrets of the din,
Of storms that roared and sweet spring days,
Of sunlit afternoons ablaze.

So gather close, let stories flow,
From bark that holds more than we know,
For in each notch and wrinkled page,
Lies laughter mixed with love and sage.

Roots That Cradle Time

The roots of wisdom stretch so wide,
While worms hold meetings deep inside,
The oak just chuckles, "Oh, what fun!"
As ants march by, a tiny army on the run.

Underneath its earthen coat,
History lingers like an old, sweet note,
Where secrets of the past take flight,
In the shadowed depths of day and night.

With every push of soil and sun,
The oak feels like it's always won,
For deep within it's never alone,
Each root a friend, a family grown.

So let us dance upon its knoll,
Where roots wrap 'round like a friendly stroll,
A party of the woodland kin,
Celebrating life beneath the skin.

Echoes of the Seasons Past

Whispers ride the autumn breeze,
As leaves drop like confetti, with ease,
The oak recalls the summers bright,
And winter's chill, a frosty bite.

Each season wears a festive hat,
A costume party for the fat,
Bark-clad chimps swing with a jest,
While nature laughs, it's simply the best.

The springtime blooms declare a truce,
And squirrels clink glasses like a moose,
To toast the raindrops soft and light,
Comedic chaos, pure delight.

So dance beneath this wooden sage,
And celebrate this lively stage,
For echoes of laughter linger long,
In the arms of nature, where we belong.

www.ingramcontent.com/pod-product-compliance
Lightning Source LLC
Chambersburg PA
CBHW071835160426
43209CB00003B/304